PIANO
Adventures® *by Nancy and Randall Faber*

_____ is sightreading this book!

(your name)

Production Coordinator: Jon Ophoff
Cover and Illustrations: Terpstra Design, San Francisco

ISBN 978-1-61677-673-2
Copyright © 2015 Dovetree Productions, Inc.
c/o FABER PIANO ADVENTURES, 3042 Creek Dr., Ann Arbor, MI 48108.
International Copyright Secured. All Rights Reserved. Printed in U.S.A.
WARNING: The music, text, design, and graphics in this publication are protected
by copyright law. Any duplication is an infringement of U.S. copyright law.

CHART YOUR PROGRESS

Sightreading for Lesson Book pp. 6–7
Aurora Borealis 6–9

☐ DAY 1 ☐ DAY 2 ☐ DAY 3 ☐ DAY 4 ☐ DAY 5

Sightreading for Lesson Book p. 9
C and Am Chord Inversions 10–13

☐ DAY 1 ☐ DAY 2 ☐ DAY 3 ☐ DAY 4 ☐ DAY 5

Sightreading for Lesson Book pp. 10–11
Maple Leaf Rag 14–17

☐ DAY 1 ☐ DAY 2 ☐ DAY 3 ☐ DAY 4 ☐ DAY 5

Sightreading for Lesson Book pp. 12–13
In the Hall of the Mountain King 18–23

☐ DAY 1 ☐ DAY 2 ☐ DAY 3 ☐ DAY 4 ☐ DAY 5

Sightreading for Lesson Book pp. 14–15
Medieval Fair 24–27

☐ DAY 1 ☐ DAY 2 ☐ DAY 3 ☐ DAY 4 ☐ DAY 5

Sightreading for Lesson Book pp. 18–19
Allegro Grazioso 28–31

☐ DAY 1 ☐ DAY 2 ☐ DAY 3 ☐ DAY 4 ☐ DAY 5

Sightreading for Lesson Book p. 21
F and Dm Chord Inversions 32–35

☐ DAY 1 ☐ DAY 2 ☐ DAY 3 ☐ DAY 4 ☐ DAY 5

Sightreading for Lesson Book pp. 22–23
Mazurka in F Major 36–39

☐ DAY 1 ☐ DAY 2 ☐ DAY 3 ☐ DAY 4 ☐ DAY 5

Sightreading for Lesson Book pp. 24–26
The Spy 40–45

☐ DAY 1 ☐ DAY 2 ☐ DAY 3 ☐ DAY 4 ☐ DAY 5

Sightreading for Lesson Book p. 27
French Minuet 46–49

☐ DAY 1 ☐ DAY 2 ☐ DAY 3 ☐ DAY 4 ☐ DAY 5

Sightreading for Lesson Book p. 29
G and Em Chord Inversions 50–53

☐ DAY 1 ☐ DAY 2 ☐ DAY 3 ☐ DAY 4 ☐ DAY 5

Sightreading for Lesson Book pp. 30–31
Grand Central Station 54–57

☐ DAY 1 ☐ DAY 2 ☐ DAY 3 ☐ DAY 4 ☐ DAY 5

SIGHTREADING SKILL

Sightreading skill is a powerful asset for the developing pianist. It makes every step of music-making easier. With the right tools and a little effort, sightreading skill can be developed to great benefit.

This book builds confident, intermediate sightreaders in these ways:

1. Recognition of the **major** or **minor key** with an understanding of its tonality; tonic, dominant, leading tone, and primary chords I-IV-V7 (or i-iv-V7).

2. Perception of common **rhythmic** and **melodic note patterns**.

3. Ability to identify chords in **root position** and **1st and 2nd inversions**.

Music reading involves more than a sequence of note names. The sightreader tracks *horizontally* and *vertically*, observing melodic and harmonic intervals, chords, rhythmic and melodic motives, dynamics, and accompaniment patterns that make up the context of the music.

This decoding skill requires repetition within familiar musical frameworks. In other words, pattern recognition develops by seeing a lot of the same patterns. Accordingly, this book presents **musical variations** to sharpen perception of the *new* against a backdrop of the *familiar*. More than any other instrumentalist, the pianist must group notes into patterns for musical understanding.

In the Level 4 Sightreading Book, these musical variations are drawn from the music introduced in the Level 4 Lesson Book—Joplin, Grieg, Lully, J.S. Bach—as well as traditional folk songs and Faber originals.

The book features the keys of D, A, and E, with their scales and primary chords, along with chord inversions and a variety of sixteenth-note patterns.

Get ready for a Level 4 Sightreading Adventure!

SIGHTREADING

How to Use

This book is organized into sets of 5 exercises for 5 days of practice. Each set provides variations on a piece from the Piano Adventures® Level 4 Lesson Book. Play one exercise a day, completing one set per week.

Though the student is not required to repeatedly "practice" the sightreading exercise, each should be repeated as indicated by the repeat sign. For an extra workout, play each of the previous exercises in the set before playing the new exercise of the day.

Curiosity and Fun

The "Don't Practice This!" motto is a bold statement which has an obvious psychological impact. It reminds us that sightreading is indeed the first time through and it reminds us to keep the activity fun.

DON'T PRACTICE THIS!

Level of Difficulty

It is most beneficial to sightread at the appropriate level of difficulty. By setting a slow, steady tempo, the student should be able to play the majority of the notes, especially on the repetition. This Piano Adventures® Sightreading Book is carefully written to provide an appropriate challenge for the Level 4 student.

Marking Progress

In previous levels, students were encouraged to draw a large **X** over each completed exercise. Due to the higher level of the student, this is now optional.

Some students may exclaim about the thickness of the book. They soon are rewarded to find how fast they can move through it. Indeed, with confidence increasing, the student can take pride in moving to completion of this very large book ... and do so with a crescendo of achievement.

Instructions to the Student

1. **Always scan the music before playing.**
   This strategy helps you "take in" the music you will be sightreading.
   You will get better and faster at "scanning" with experience.

2. **Scan the basics first.**

   - What is the key? Major or minor?

   - What is the time signature?

   - What measures look difficult? Mentally hear them before playing.
     You may wish to tap the rhythm lightly in your lap.

   - Now look for patterns. Are there any measures that repeat? How many?

   - Can you spot I, IV, or V7 chords?

   - Scan for scale passages and thumb-crossings. Any hand shifts?

   - Now scan for dynamics, sharps, flats, naturals, and rests.

3. **Count-off the tempo.**

   - Set a slow, steady tempo of two measures and begin to play.
     You may need to subdivide the count-off: "1 e + a 2 e + a," etc.

   - You may enjoy drawing a big X through the music to show completion.

DAY 1: Aurora Borealis

Key of ____ Major

Scan the music. Notice where the R.H. patterns change.
Prepare your right foot on the pedal.

DAY 2: Aurora Borealis

Key of ___ Major

Scan the music for R.H. pattern changes.
Silently finger the L.H. bass notes.

DAY 3: Aurora Borealis

Key of ___ Major

Scan the music.
Notice that the pattern changes in each measure.

DON'T PRACTICE THIS!

DAY 4: Aurora Borealis

Key of ____ Major

Notice the L.H. cross-over notes.
Plan how you will play each one.

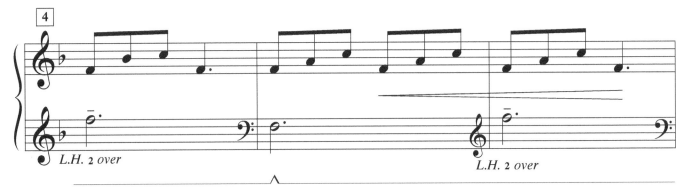

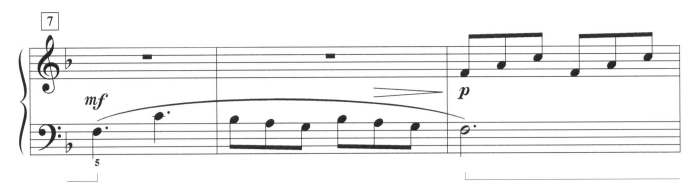

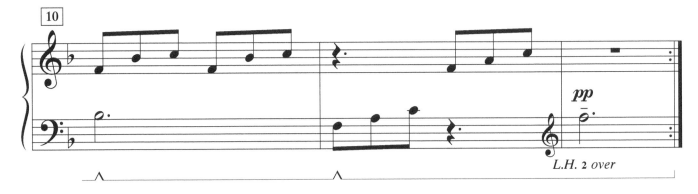

DAY 5: Aurora Borealis

Key of ____ Major

Scan the music for R.H. pattern changes.
Silently finger the L.H. bass notes.

DAY 1: C and Am Chord Inversions

Key of C Major

Scan the music for R.H. chord inversion shifts.
Silently play them before sightreading.

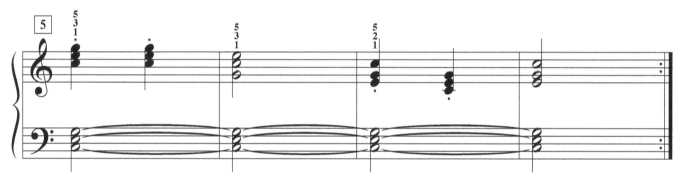

DAY 2: C and Am Chord Inversions

Key of C Major
(for L.H. alone)

Scan the music for L.H. chord inversion shifts.
Silently play them before sightreading.

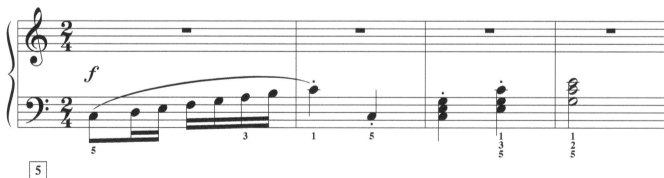

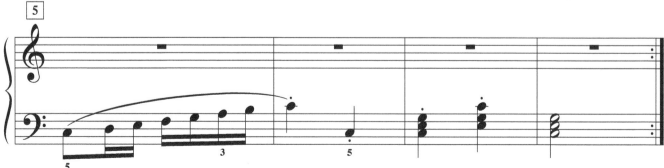

DAY 3: C and Am Chord Inversions

Key of ____ Major / Minor (circle)

Scan the music. Which minor scale is played?

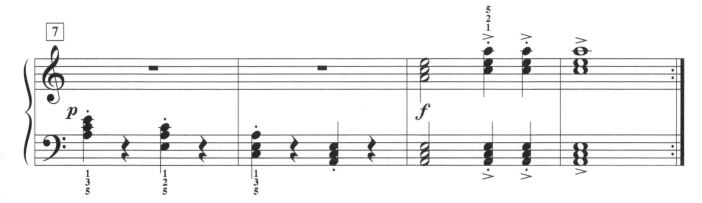

Label each example as C major (C) or A minor (Am).

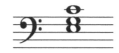

DAY 4: C and Am Chord Inversions

Key of ____ Major/Minor

Scan the music. Where do lines 1, 2, and 4 change from C major to A minor chords? Sightread s-l-o-w-l-y, preparing each chord.

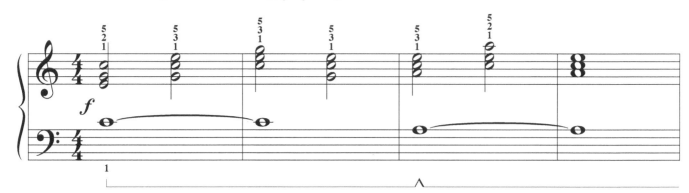

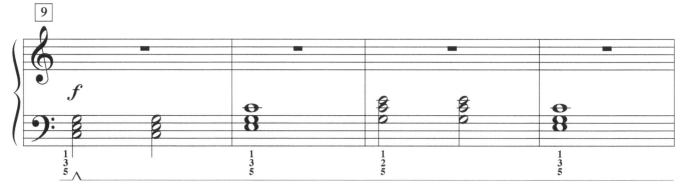

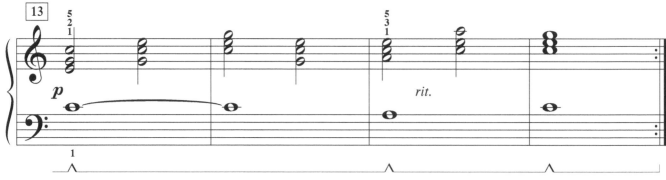

DAY 5: C and Am Chord Inversions

Key of ____ Major/Minor

DON'T PRACTICE THIS!

Scan the music. What broken chord is played?
Mentally hear the dotted rhythm in measures 9–11 before sightreading.

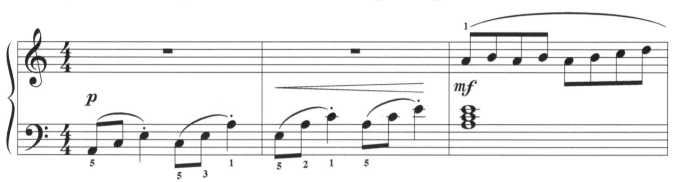

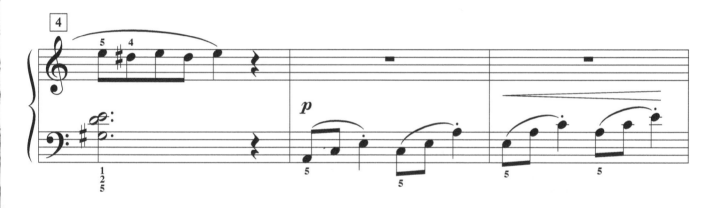

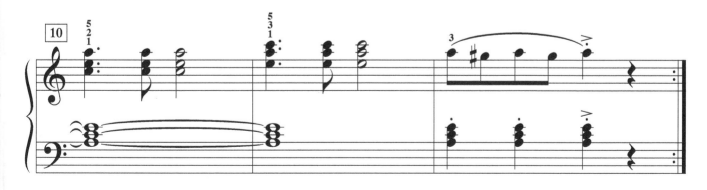

DAY 1: Maple Leaf Rag

Key of ____ Major/Minor

DON'T PRACTICE THIS!

Silently finger the I–V7 chords for measures 1–2.

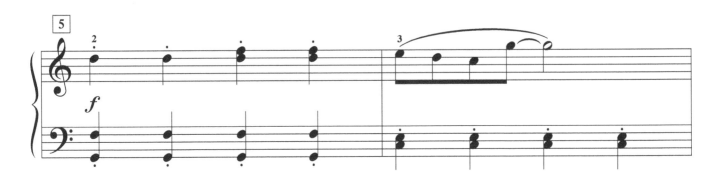

DAY 2: Maple Leaf Rag

Key of ____ Major/Minor

Scan the music. Silently finger the R.H. chord inversions
in measures 5–6.

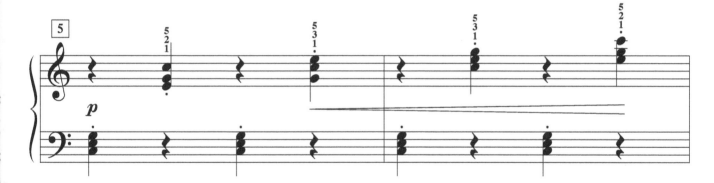

DAY 3: Maple Leaf Rag

Key of ____ Major/Minor

Scan the music. Where does the L.H. shift quickly to the V7 (G7) chord?

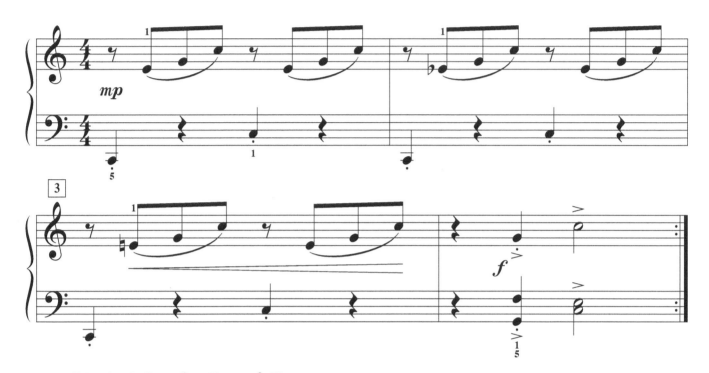

DAY 4: Maple Leaf Rag

Key of ____ Major/Minor
(for L.H. alone)

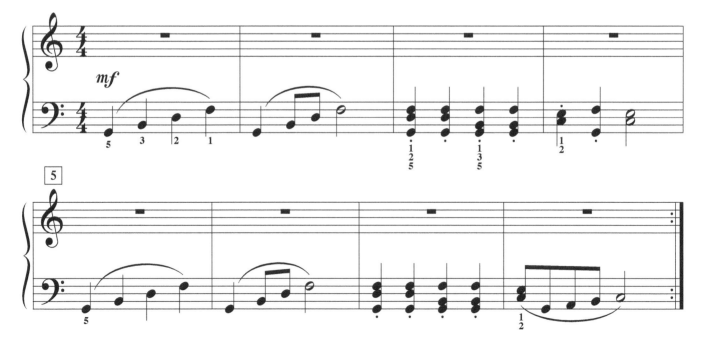

DAY 5: Maple Leaf Rag

Key of ____ Major/Minor

Scan the music. Plan how you will play each L.H. chord change.

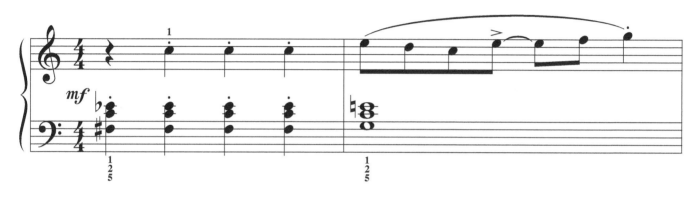

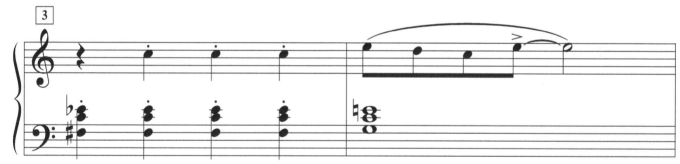

DAY 1: In the Hall of the Mountain King

Key of ____ Major/Minor

Where does the music shift to C major?

DON'T PRACTICE THIS!

SIGHTREADING

DAY 2: In the Hall of the Mountain King

Key of ____ Major/Minor

DON'T PRACTICE THIS!

In which two measures is it important to count the half rest?

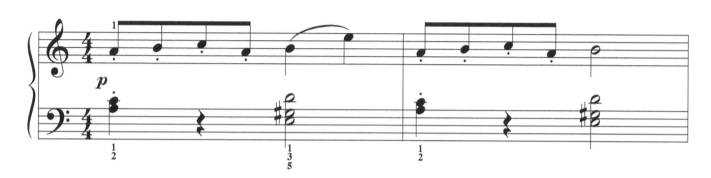

DAY 3: In the Hall of the Mountain King

Key of ____ Major/Minor
(for L.H. alone)

Which scale is played at measure 4? Plan how you will play it.

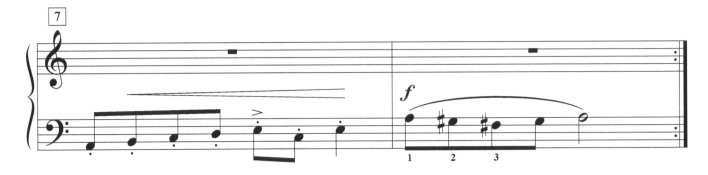

DAY 4: In the Hall of the Mountain King

Key of ____ Major/Minor

Scan the music and notice each hand position change.
Where do you play a L.H. V7 (E7) chord? Plan how you will play it.

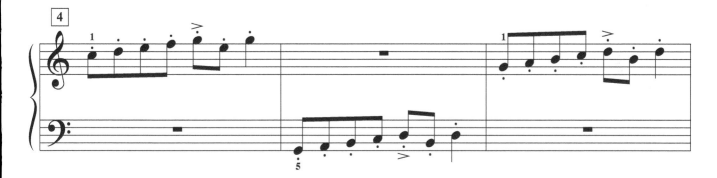

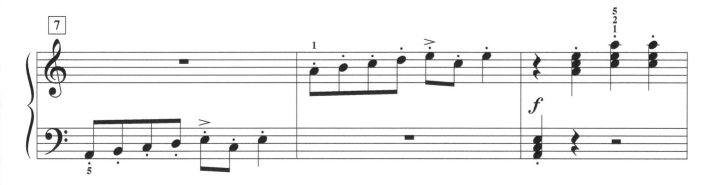

DAY 5: In the Hall of the Mountain King

Key of ___ Major/Minor

What form of the minor scale is shown at measures 3–4?

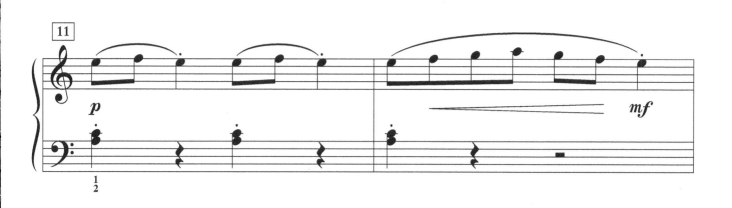

Circle each E7 chord. Hint: There are four.

SIGHTREADING

based on Lesson Book pp. 14–15

DAY 1: Medieval Fair

Key of ____ Major/Minor

Scan the music. Notice the hand position changes.
Mentally hear the rhythm of the opening before playing.

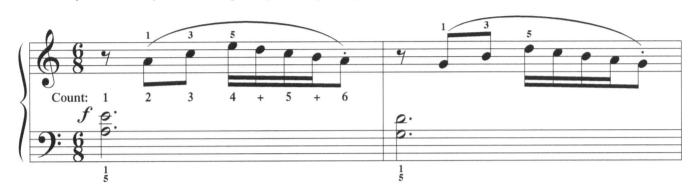

Count: 1   2   3   4   +   5   +   6

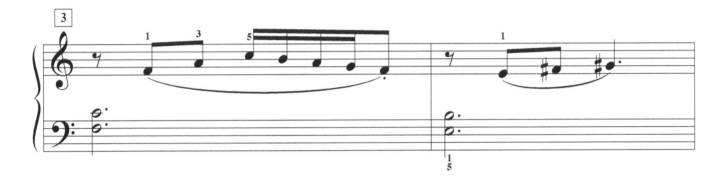

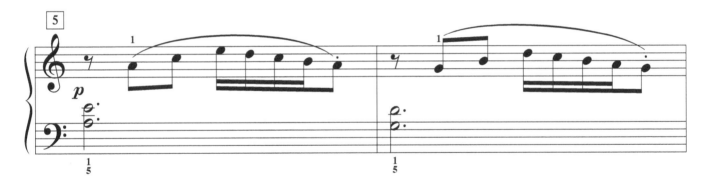

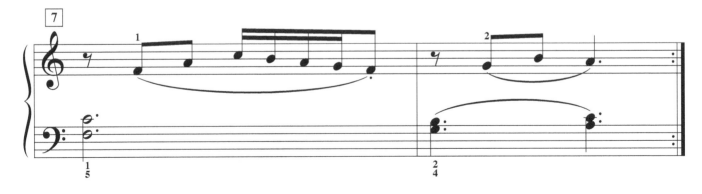

24

DAY 2: Medieval Fair

Key of ____ Major/Minor

Mentally hear the rhythm of the opening before playing.

DAY 3: Medieval Fair

Key of ____ Major/Minor
(for L.H. alone)

DAY 4: Medieval Fair

Key of ____ Major/Minor

DON'T PRACTICE THIS!

Scan the music and notice each L.H. position change.

DAY 5: Medieval Fair

Key of ____ Major/Minor

DON'T PRACTICE THIS!

Which measures use broken chords? Which measures use scales?
Scan the music for each hand position change.

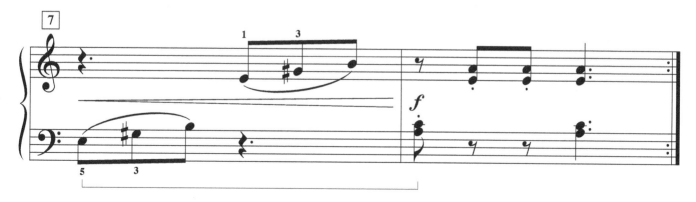

DAY 1: Allegro Grazioso

Key of ____ Major/Minor

The L.H. plays I and V7 harmony.
Silently finger the L.H. before sightreading.

DAY 2: Allegro Grazioso

Key of ____ Major/Minor
(for L.H. alone)

DAY 3: Allegro Grazioso

Key of ____ Major/Minor

DON'T
PRACTICE
THIS!

Notice the L.H. begins in the treble clef!

DAY 4: Allegro Grazioso

Key of _____ Major/Minor

What two chords does the L.H. play?

Draw bar lines for this 2/4 rhythm.
Can you tap while counting 1 e + a 2 e + a ?

DAY 5: Allegro Grazioso

Key of ___ Major/Minor

Notice the L.H. begins in the treble clef!

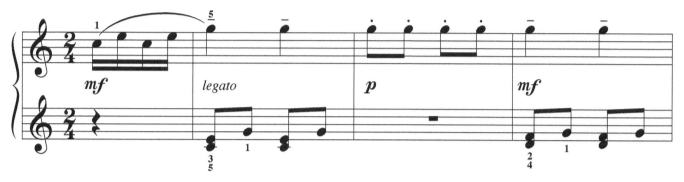

DAY 1: F and Dm Chord Inversions
Key of F Major

Scan the music for chord changes from F major to D minor.

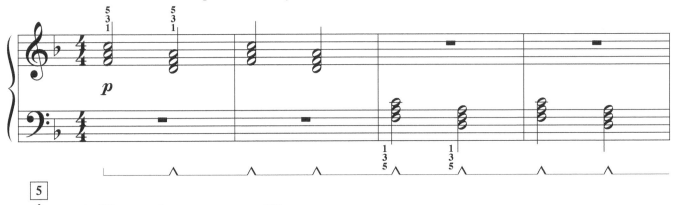

DAY 2: F and Dm Chord Inversions
Key of F Major

Scan the music for chord inversion changes.

DAY 3: F and Dm Chord Inversions

Key of ____ Major/Minor

Silently finger the opening R.H. scale.

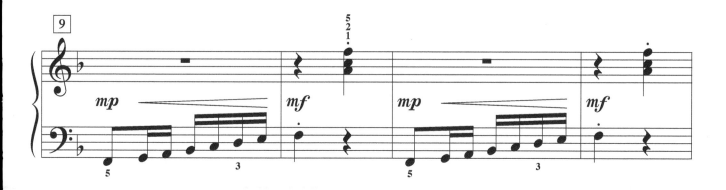

DAY 4: F and Dm Chord Inversions

Key of ____ Major/Minor

Scan the music for chord inversion changes.

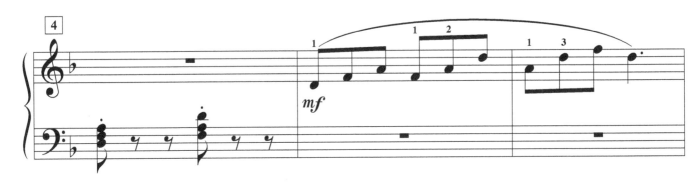

Label each example as F major (F) or D minor (Dm).

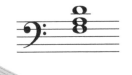   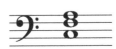 

DAY 5: F and Dm Chord Inversions

Key of _____ Major/Minor

Shape each phrase with a crescendo and diminuendo.

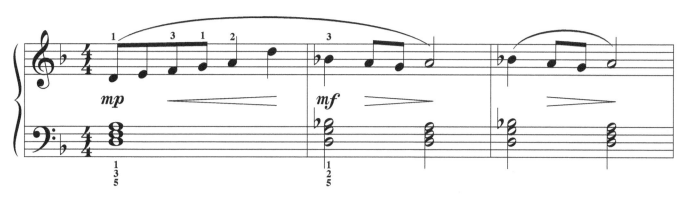

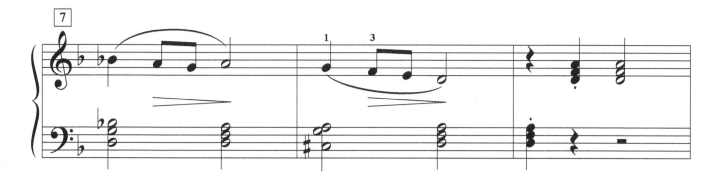

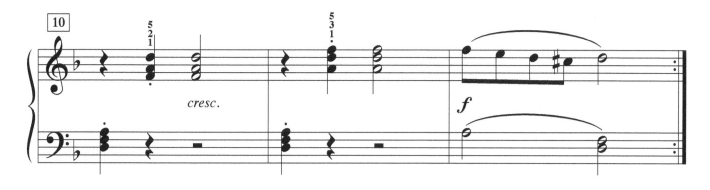

DAY 1: Mazurka in F Major

Plan the F and C7 (I and V7) chords before sightreading.

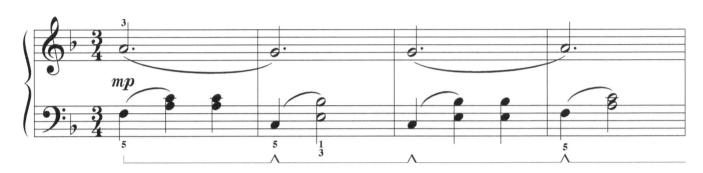

SIGHTREADING

DAY 2: Mazurka in F Major

Where does the ♪♫ ♩ pattern change to a triplet?

DAY 3: Mazurka in F Major

Plan how you will play measure 2 before sightreading.
Remember the B♭!

DAY 4: Mazurka in F Major

Scan the music. Where does the L.H. play the root position C7 (V7) chord?
Silently finger it before sightreading.

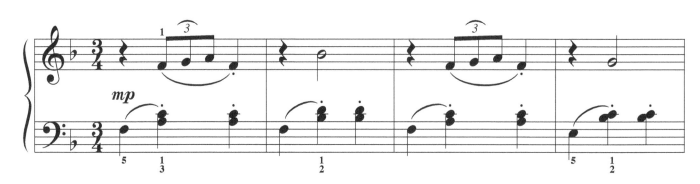

Draw bar lines for this 3/4 rhythm.
Can you tap while counting 1 e + a 2 e + a 3 e + a ?

38

DAY 5: Mazurka in F Major

Plan the F and C7 (I and V7) chords before sightreading.

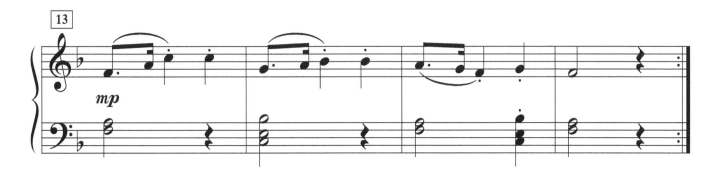

DAY 1: The Spy

Key of _____ Major/Minor

Before sightreading, silently finger the R.H. chords,
and then the opening L.H. measures. Notice the L.H. pattern.

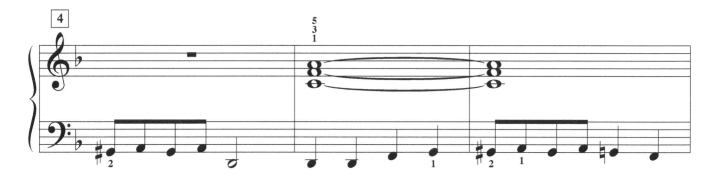

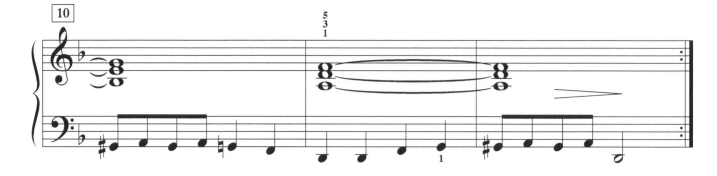

DAY 2: The Spy
Key of ___ Major/Minor

DON'T PRACTICE THIS!

Scan the music for patterns for each hand.

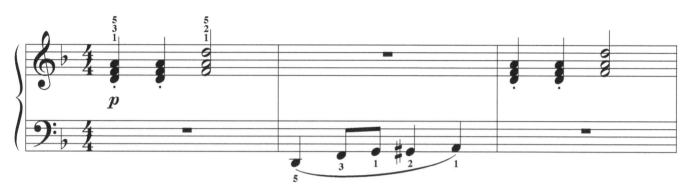

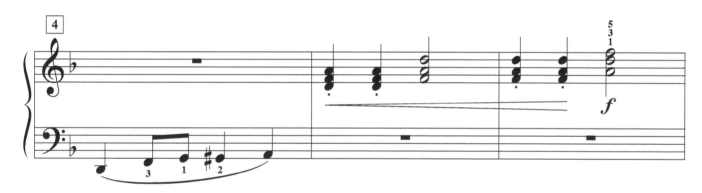

Label each D minor chord as root, 1st inversion (1st inv.), or 2nd inversion (2nd inv.).

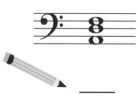

___   ___   ___   ___   ___

DAY 3: The Spy

Key of ___ Major/Minor
(for L.H. alone)

This music opens with a L.H. broken A7 chord.
Plan how you will play it.

SIGHTREADING

DAY 4: The Spy
Key of ___ Major/Minor

DON'T
PRACTICE
THIS!

Mentally hear the opening rhythm before sightreading.

DAY 5: The Spy

Key of ____ Major/Minor

Silently finger measure 1.
Notice how many times this pattern repeats!

DAY 1: French Minuet

Key of ____ Major/Minor

DON'T PRACTICE THIS!

Notice the R.H. crossover to C♯ in the opening melodic pattern.

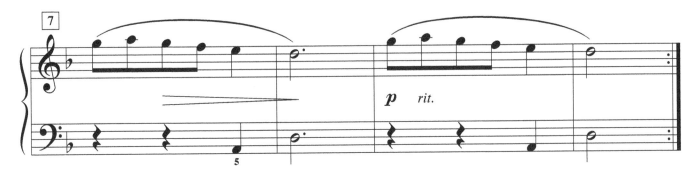

Identify each minor scale as natural or harmonic.

DAY 2: French Minuet
Key of ___ Major/Minor
(for L.H. alone)

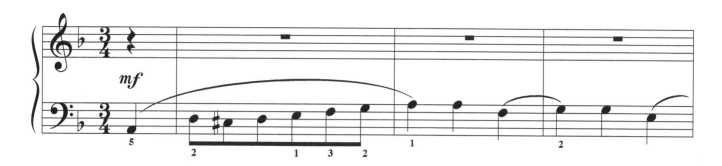

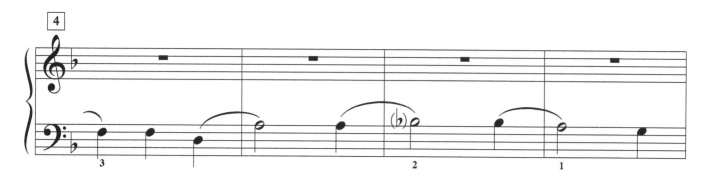

DAY 3: French Minuet

Key of ____ Major/Minor

Notice the accidentals in the melodic pattern for each hand.

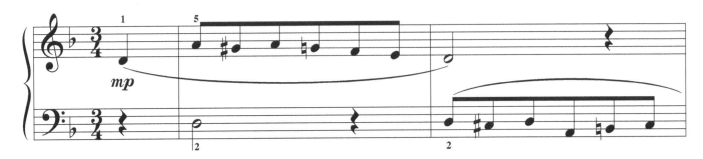

DAY 4: French Minuet

Key of ____ Major/Minor

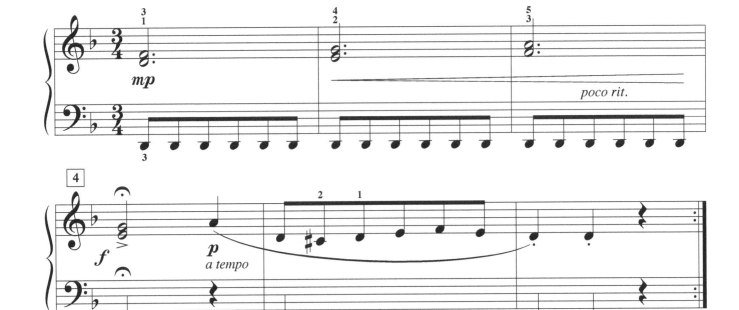

DAY 5: French Minuet

Key of ___ Major/Minor

Plan the Dm and A7 (i and V7) chords before sightreading.

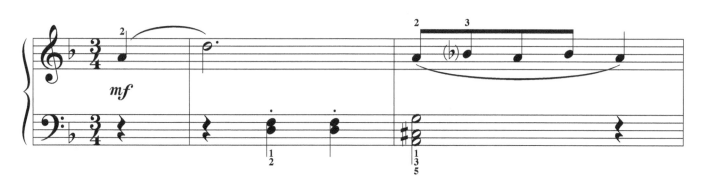

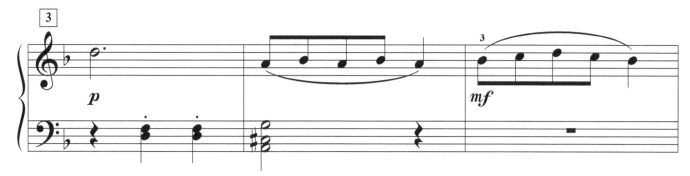

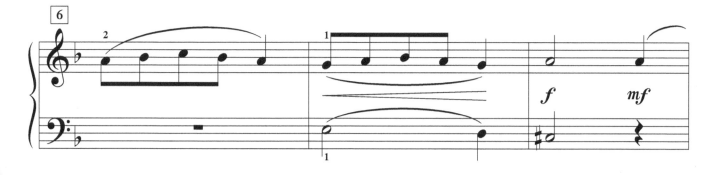

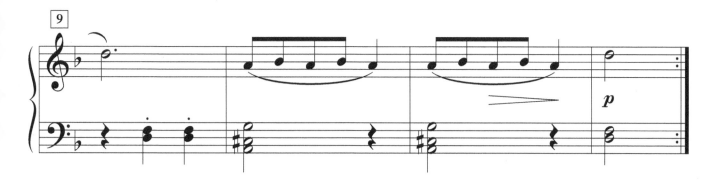

DAY 1: G and Em Chord Inversions

Key of ____ Major/Minor

Scan the music for R.H. chord inversion shifts.
What style of accompaniment does the L.H. play?

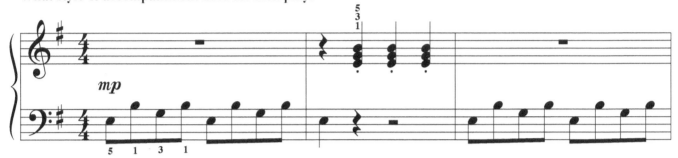

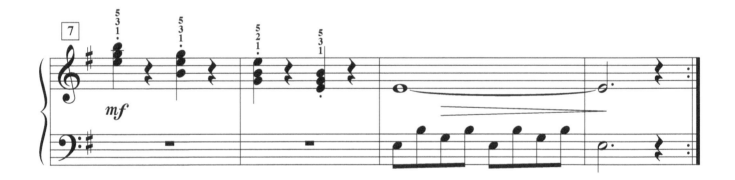

Label each example as G major (G) or E minor (Em).

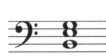

DAY 2: G and Em Chord Inversions
Key of ____ Major/Minor

DAY 3: G and Em Chord Inversions
Key of ____ Major/Minor

Scan the music for chord changes from G major to E minor.

DAY 4: G and Em Chord Inversions

Key of ___ Major/Minor

Plan how you will play the L.H. chord inversions.

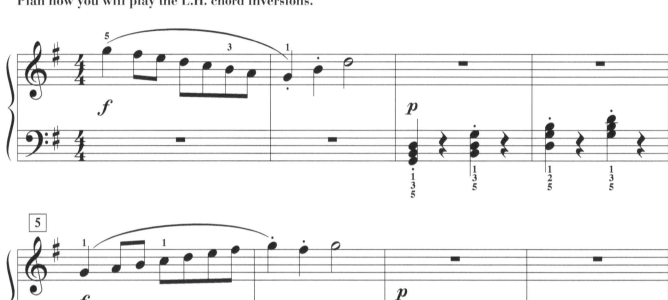

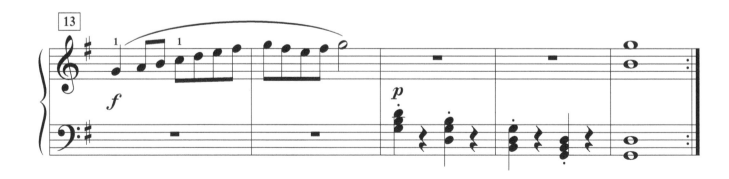

DAY 5: G and Em Chord Inversions

Key of ____ Major/Minor

Plan how you will play the L.H. chord inversions.

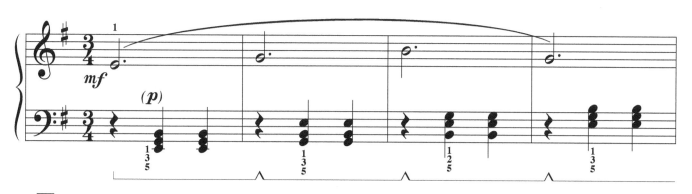

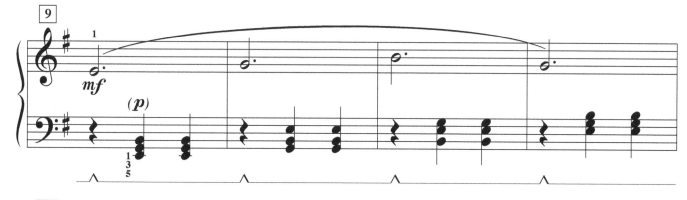

DAY 1: Grand Central Station

Key of _____ Major/Minor

Plan how you will play the rhythm pattern from measures 9–12.

SIGHTREADING

DAY 2: Grand Central Station

Key of ___ Major/Minor

Silently finger the L.H. octaves before sightreading.

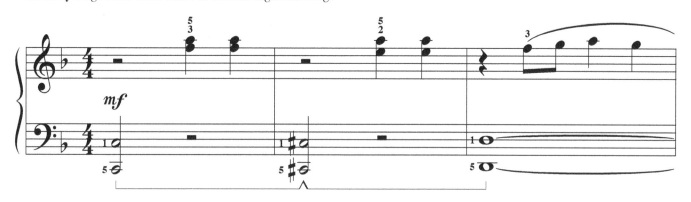

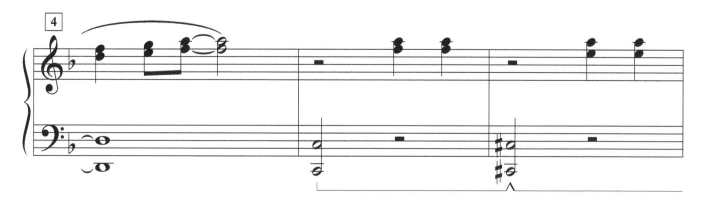

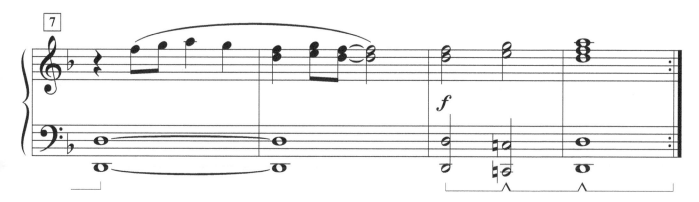

Tap this two-handed rhythm while counting aloud: 1 + 2 + 3 + 4 +

DAY 3: Grand Central Station

Key of ____ Major/Minor

Name the R.H. intervals and silently finger them.
Notice the changing L.H. 5ths in each measure.

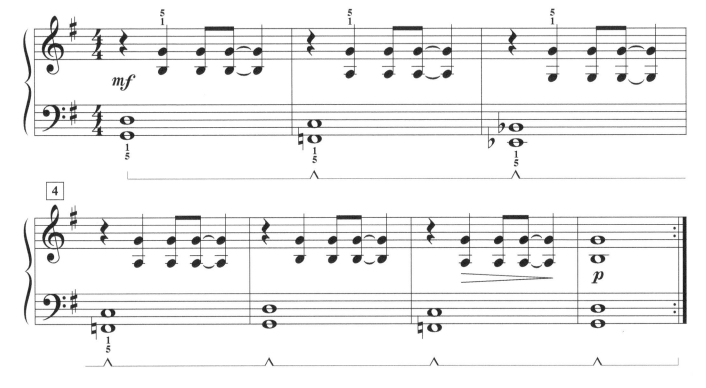

DAY 4: Grand Central Station

Key of ____ Major/Minor

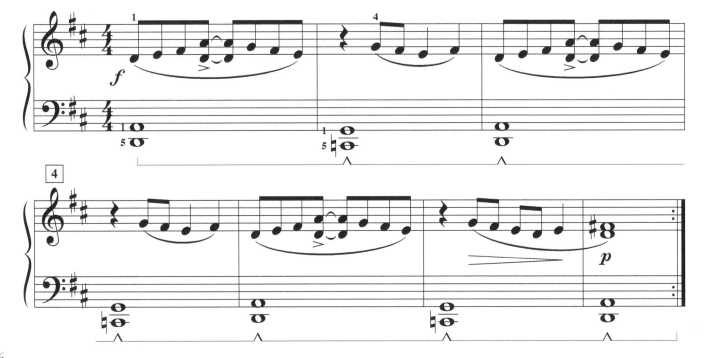

DAY 5: Grand Central Station

Key of ____ Major/Minor

Notice the time signature. Scan the music for note changes in the R.H. pattern.

57

DAY 1: Volga Boatmen

Key of _____ Major/Minor

Scan the music. Notice the use of R.H. triplets.
What two intervals does the L.H. use?

Draw an X through each incorrect measure in 4/4 time.

DAY 2: Volga Boatmen

Key of ____ Major/Minor

Silently finger the R.H. scale in measure 7 before sightreading.

DAY 3: Volga Boatmen

Key of _____ Major/Minor

Scan the music for R.H. chord inversion shifts.

Circle each D minor chord. Hint: There are four.

DAY 4: Volga Boatmen

Key of ____ Major/Minor

DON'T PRACTICE THIS!

Plan the Em and B7 (i and V7) chords before sightreading.

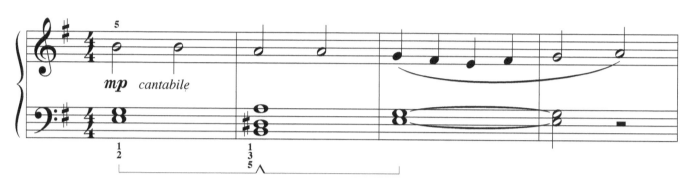

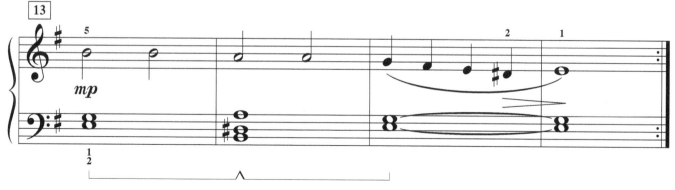

DAY 5: Volga Boatmen

Key of ____ Major/Minor

Scan the music for these three L.H. chords: B7, Em, and C.

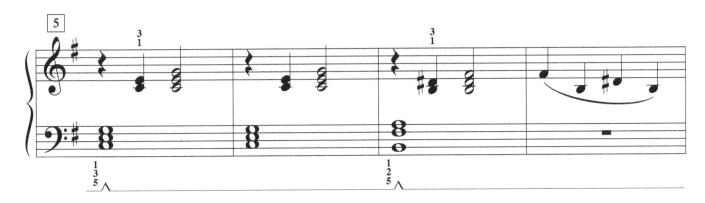

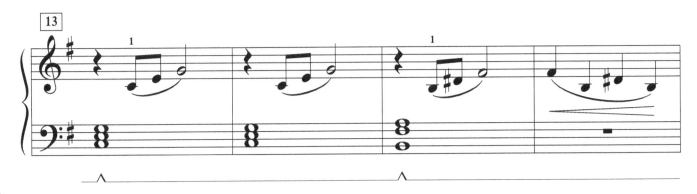

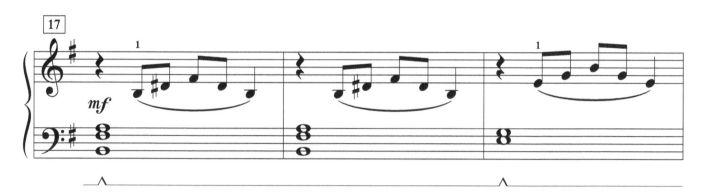

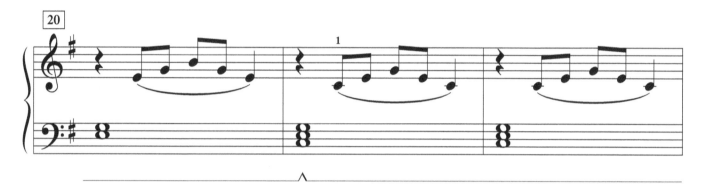

Circle each B7 chord. Hint: There are four.

DAY 1: Bourée

Key of _____ Major/Minor

DON'T PRACTICE THIS!

Scan the music. Try mentally hearing the R.H. melody before you play.

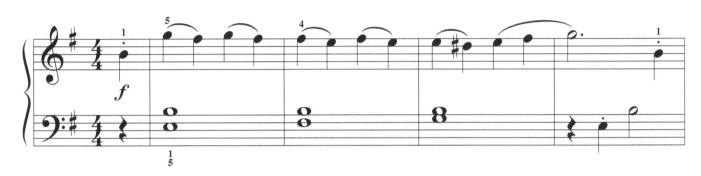

Name the major and minor key for each key signature below.

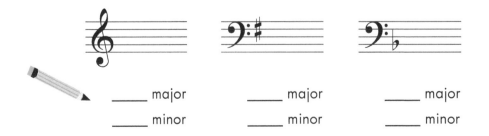

_____ major
_____ minor

_____ major
_____ minor

_____ major
_____ minor

DAY 2: Bourée

Key of ___ Major/Minor
  (for L.H. alone)

Silently finger the opening four measures before sightreading.

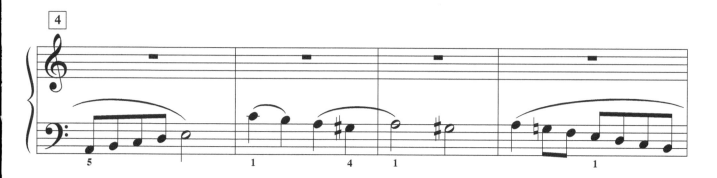

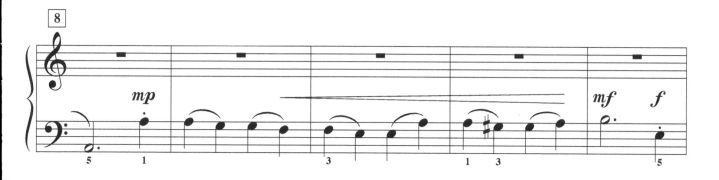

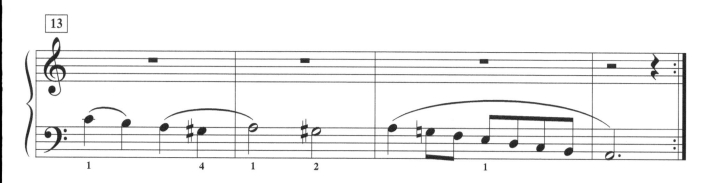

DAY 3: Bourée

Key of ____ Major/Minor

Prepare your L.H. over the opening notes before sightreading.

DAY 4: Bourée

Key of ____ Major/Minor

DAY 5: Bourée

Key of ___ Major/Minor

Notice the two voices for the R.H. in measures 7 and 15.

DON'T PRACTICE THIS!

DAY 1: Chanson

Key of ____ Major/Minor

Silently finger the L.H. patterns before sightreading.

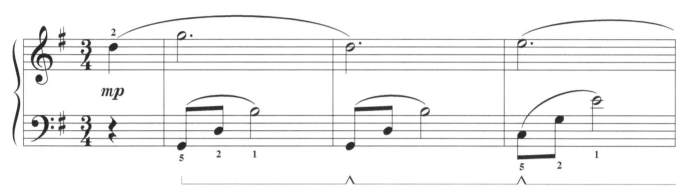

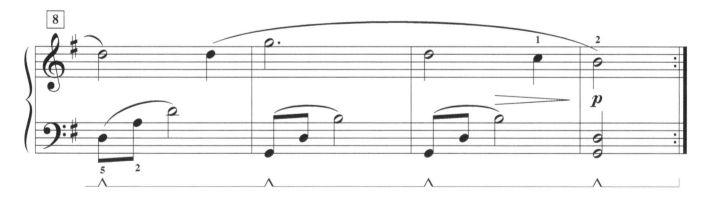

Write the chord symbol for each example (G, B7, etc.).

____   ____   ____   ____

DAY 2: Chanson

Key of ___ Major/Minor

Plan the hand position changes for the L.H. before sightreading.

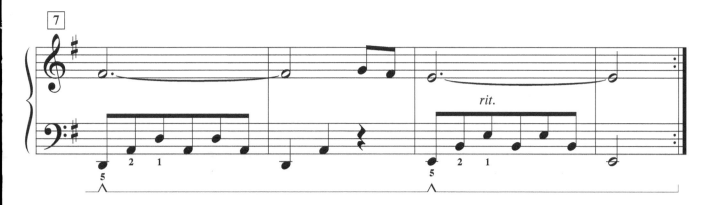

Tap this two-handed rhythm while counting aloud: 1 + 2 + 3 +

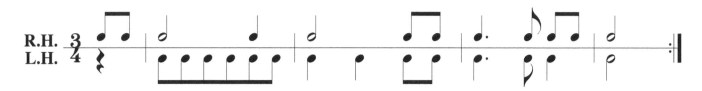

R.H. L.H.

DAY 3: Chanson

Key of ____ Major/Minor

DON'T PRACTICE THIS!

DAY 4: Chanson

**Key of ____ Major/Minor
(for L.H. alone)**

Plan the hand position changes for the L.H. before sightreading.

DAY 5: Chanson

Key of _____ Major/Minor

Plan the hand position changes for the L.H. before sightreading.

DAY 1: Two-Octave Major Scales

Key of ____ Major

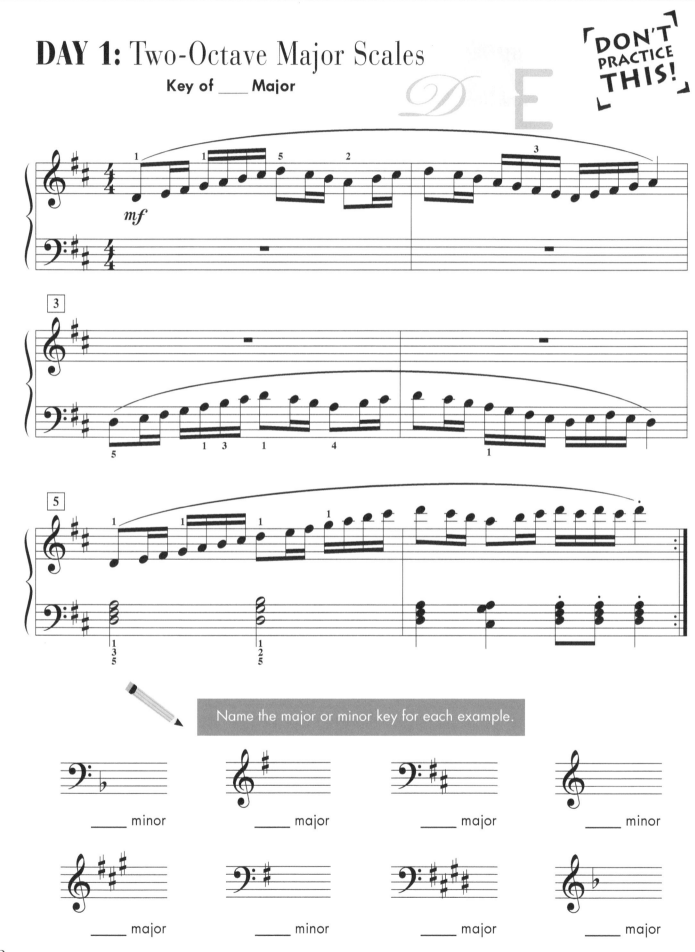

Name the major or minor key for each example.

____ minor   ____ major   ____ major   ____ minor

____ major   ____ minor   ____ major   ____ major

SIGHTREADING

DAY 2: Two-Octave Major Scales

Key of _____ Major

DAY 3: Two-Octave Major Scales

Key of ___ Major

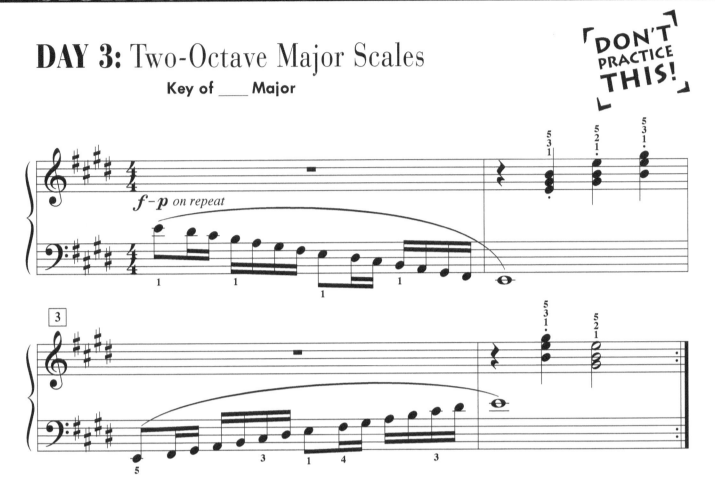

DAY 4: Two-Octave Major Scales

Key of ___ Major

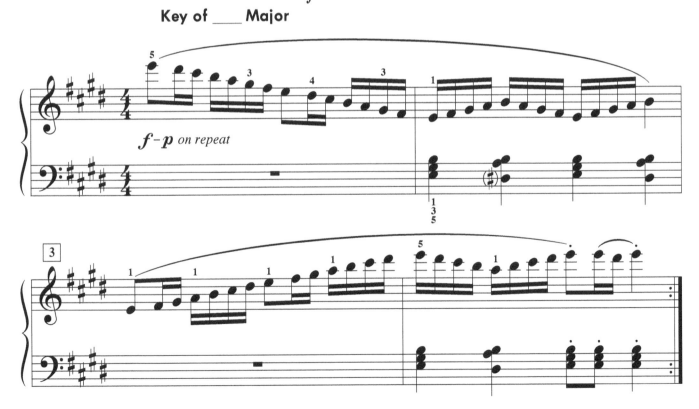

DAY 5: Two-Octave Major Scales

Key of _____ Major

Silently play the R.H. scale passage for measures 5-8.
Where are the sharps?

DON'T PRACTICE THIS!

DAY 1: Ceremony for Peace

Key of ____ Major/Minor

DON'T PRACTICE THIS!

Scan the music for R.H. chord inversion shifts.
Feel the rhythm for measures 1-2. Did you mentally hear the triplet?

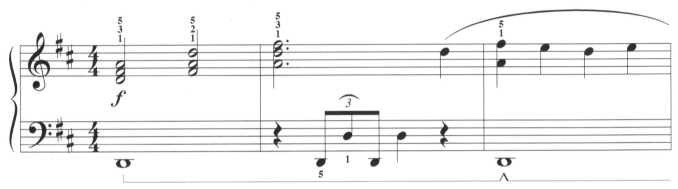

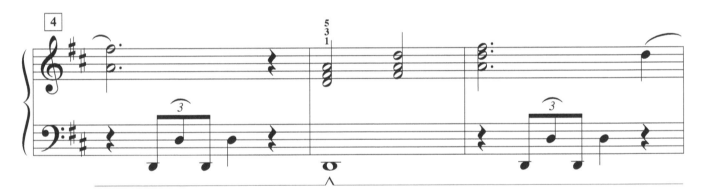

Name each interval (2nd, 3rd, 4th, 5th, 6th, 7th, 8ve).

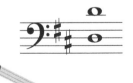

DAY 2: Ceremony for Peace

Key of ____ Major/Minor

Scan the music for R.H. chord inversion shifts.

DAY 3: Ceremony for Peace

Key of D Major

Silently finger the rhythm for measures 1-2 before playing.

DAY 4: Ceremony for Peace

Key of D Major

Plan how you will play the L.H. pattern and the shifts of that pattern.

DAY 5: Ceremony for Peace

Key of ___ Major/Minor

Scan the music for R.H. chord inversion shifts.
Before playing, think the rhythm for measures 1-3, including the L.H. triplets.

DAY 1: Gigue

Key of ____ Major

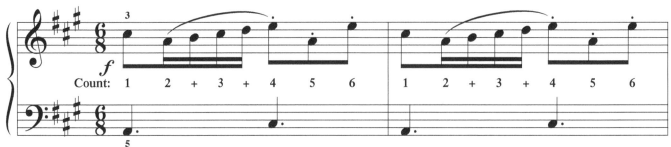

Mentally hear the opening rhythm
before sightreading.

DON'T
PRACTICE
THIS!

Count: 1   2   +   3   +   4   5   6   1   2   +   3   +   4   5   6

SIGHTREADING

DAY 2: Gigue

Key of ___ Major
(for L.H. alone)

Silently finger the notes for measures 1-2.

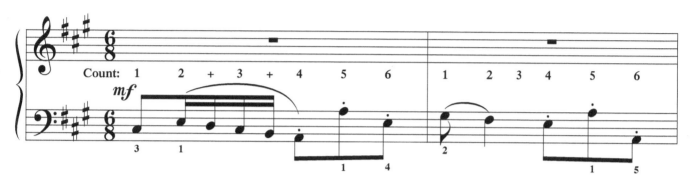

DAY 3: Gigue

Key of ____ Major

DON'T
PRACTICE
THIS!

Notice the key signature.
Silently finger the notes for measures 1-2. Notice the octaves!

DAY 4: Gigue

Key of ____ Major

DON'T
PRACTICE
THIS!

Notice the key signature.
Silently finger the notes for measures 1-2. Notice the accidentals.

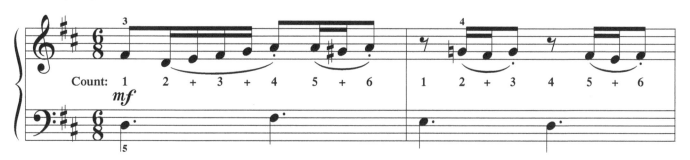

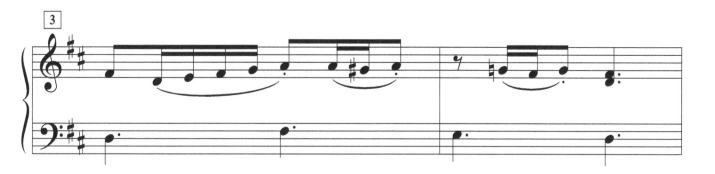

Draw bar lines for this 6/8 rhythm.
Can you tap while counting 1 + 2 + 3 + 4 + 5 + 6 + ?

DAY 5: Gigue

Key of ___ Major

Scan the music slowly. Notice the rhythm patterns.
Take note of hand position shifts starting at measure 9.

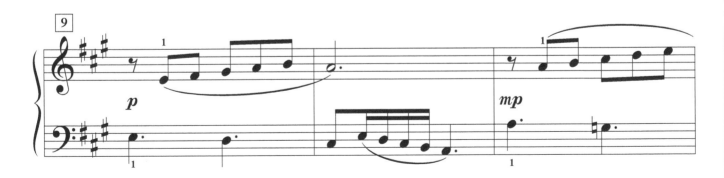

Circle the measures with 6 beats.

DAY 1: Great Barrier Reef

Key of ____ Major

DON'T PRACTICE THIS!

Scan the L.H. notes. Is there a change in pitch?
Notice the R.H. chord changes every two measures. Plan how you will play the changes.

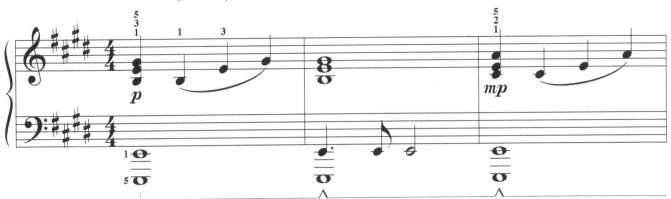

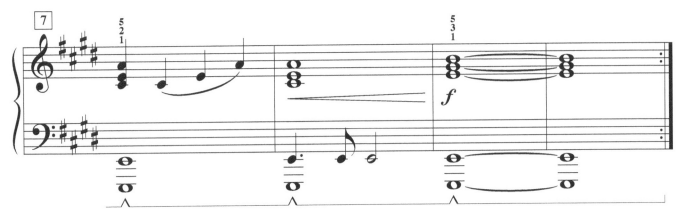

Circle each E major chord. Hint: There are three.

DAY 2: Great Barrier Reef

Key of _____ Major

Mentally hear the rhythm of measures 1–2 before sightreading.

DAY 3: Great Barrier Reef

Key of _____ Major

DON'T PRACTICE THIS!

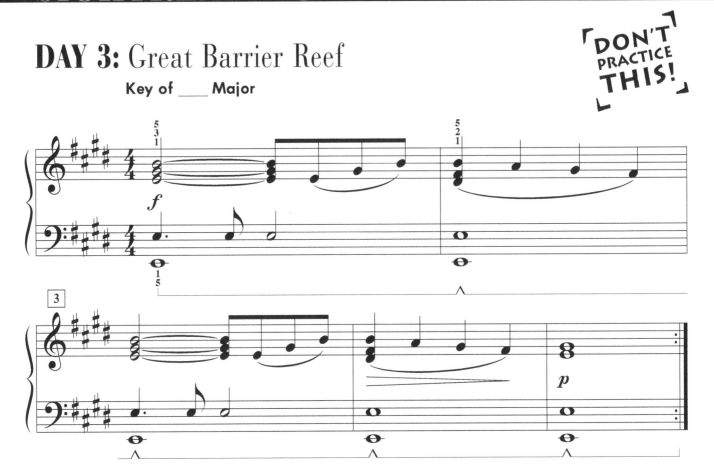

DAY 4: Great Barrier Reef

Key of _____ Major
(for L.H. alone)

Silently finger the scale at measures 5-6 before sightreading. Think sharps!

DAY 5: Great Barrier Reef

Key of _____ Major

DON'T PRACTICE THIS!

Scan the music. Silently play the L.H. octave changes.
Scan the music again. Silently play the R.H. chord changes.

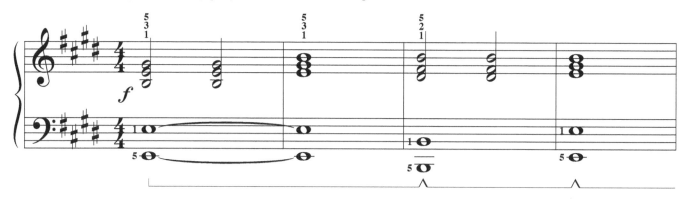

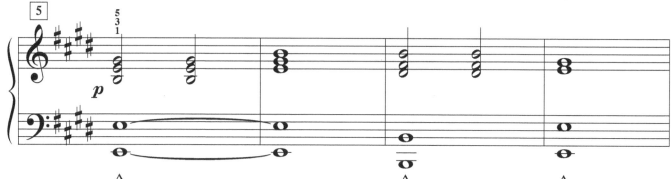

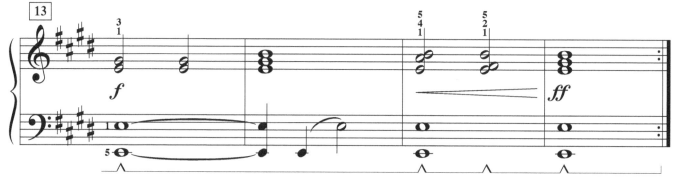

DAY 1: Prelude in C

Scan the music slowly. Notice the rhythm pattern
used throughout. Silently finger the chord changes.

Count: 1 e + a 2 e + a 3 e + a 4 e + a

Can you circle the incorrect measure in 4/4 time?

DAY 2: Prelude in C

DON'T PRACTICE THIS!

Mentally hear the rhythm pattern of measure 1 before playing.
Silently finger the R.H. chord inversion changes in measures 5-6.

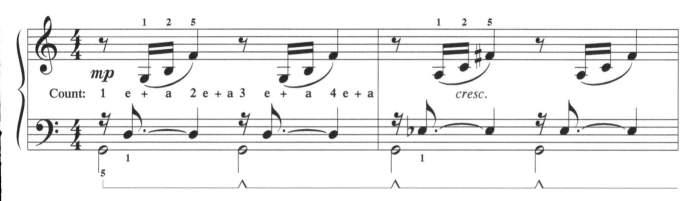

Tap this two-handed rhythm while counting aloud: 1 e + a 2 e + a 3 e + a 4 e + a

91

DAY 3: Prelude in C

DON'T PRACTICE THIS!

Set a slow, steady beat. Always look ahead to prepare
the next chord change.

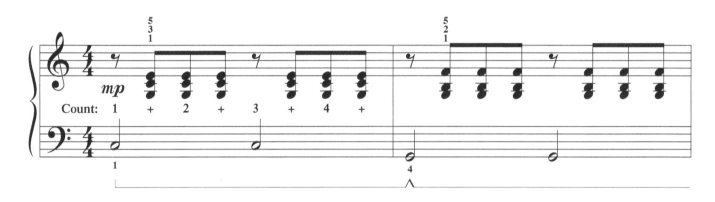

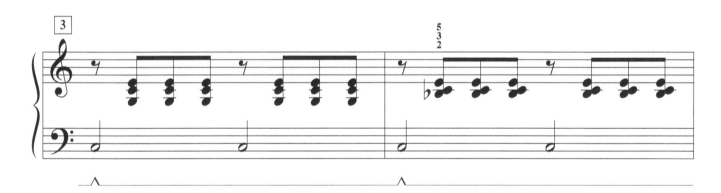

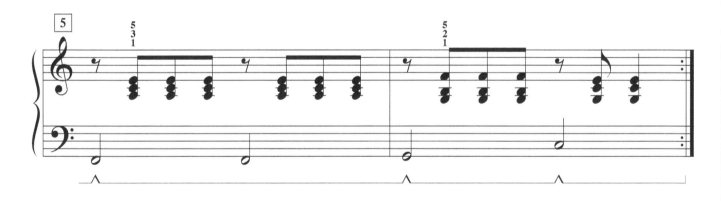

Create two measures of your own 4/4 rhythm. Use 16th-note patterns.
How complex can you be?

4/4

SIGHTREADING

DAY 4: Prelude in C

Set a slow beat to sightread these chords.
Keep looking ahead!

SIGHTREADING

DAY 5: Prelude in C

DON'T
PRACTICE
THIS!

Take a moment to scan the music.
Notice the entire piece is based on the rhythm pattern of measure 1.

Count: 1 e + a 2 e + a 3 + 4 +

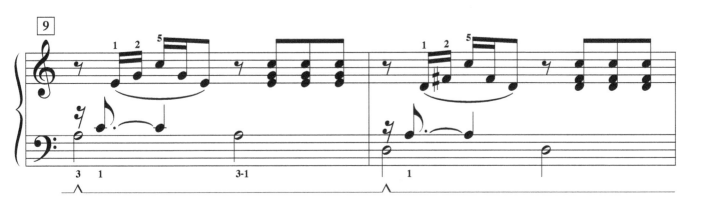

Piano Adventures® Certificate

CONGRATULATIONS

_____

(Your Name)

You are now a Level 4 Sightreader.
Keep up the great work!

_____

Teacher

_____

Date